PRESENTED BY

A Friend

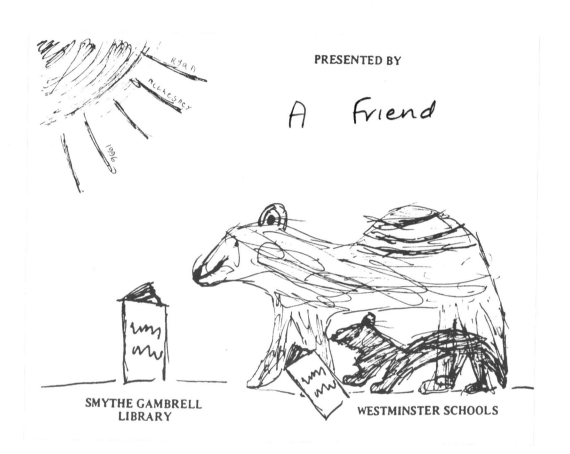

SMYTHE GAMBRELL
LIBRARY

WESTMINSTER SCHOOLS

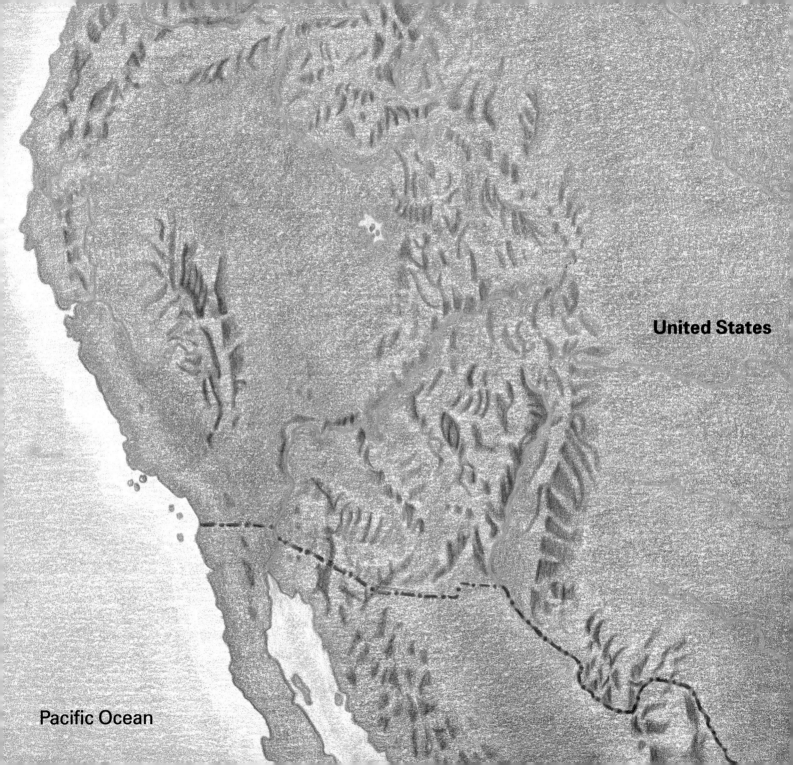

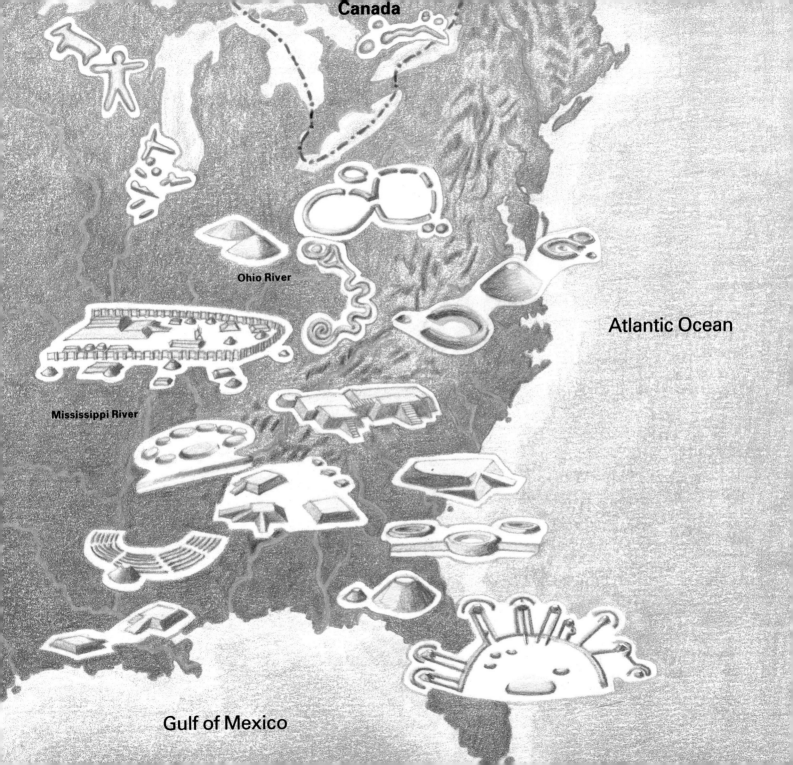

Canada

Ohio River

Atlantic Ocean

Mississippi River

Gulf of Mexico

Native sites: the Southeast

Bonnie Shemie

Mounds of earth and shell

Tundra Books

Published in Canada by Tundra Books, Montreal, Quebec H3Z 2N2

Published in the United States by Tundra Books of Northern New York, Plattsburgh, N.Y. 12901

Distributed in the United Kingdom by Ragged Bears Ltd., Andover, Hampshire SP11 9HX

Library of Congress Number: 93-60335

Canadian Cataloging in Publication Data

Shemie, Bonnie, 1949 -
    Mounds of earth and shell

ISBN 0-88776-318-9 hardcover   5 4 3 2 1

1. Mounds – North America. 2. Indians of North America – Antiquities. I. Title.

E73.S53 1993   970.01   C93-090205-X

Design by Rolf Harder

Printed in Hong Kong by the South China Printing Co. (1988) Ltd.

Also by Bonnie Shemie:
Houses of snow, skin and bones: Native dwellings of the Far North
Houses of bark: Native dwellings of the woodland Indians
Houses of hide and earth: Native dwellings of the Plains
Houses of wood: Native dwellings of the Northwest Coast

Acknowledgements:

The author/illustrator wishes to thank the McCord Museum and the libraries of McGill University, Montreal; and Dr. J. Daniel Rogers, Associate Curator of Anthropology at the National Museum of Natural History, Smithsonian Institution, Washington, D.C. for his helpful comments and suggestions.

Bibliography:

Fundaburke, Emma Lila, *Southeastern Indian Life Portraits: A Catalogue of Pictures, 1564-1860*, New Jersey: Scarecrow Reprint Corp., 1969.

Fundaburke, Emma Lila, *Sun Circles and Human Hands; The Southeastern Indians Art and Industries*, Luverne: Published by Emma Lila Fundaburke, 1957.

Hudson, Charles, *The Southeastern Indians*, Knoxville: University of Tennessee Press, 1976.

Kenyon, W.A., *Mounds of Sacred Earth: Burial Mounds of Ontario*, Toronto: The Royal Ontario Museum, 1986.

Korp, Maureen, *The Sacred Geography of the American Mound Builders*, Lewiston: Edwin Mellen Press, 1990.

Le Page du Pratz, *The History of Louisiana*, Baton Rouge: Claitor's Publishing Division, first published in 1758.

McDonald, Jerry N. and Woodward, Susan L., *Indian Mounds of the Atlantic Coast*, Newark: McDonald and Woodward Publishing Company, 1987.

Morgan, William, *Prehistoric Architecture in the Eastern United States*, Cambridge: MIT Press, 1980.

Nabokov, Peter and Easton, Robert, *Native American Architecture*, New York: Oxford University Press, 1989.

Phillips, Philip and Brown, James A., *Pre-Columbian Shell Engravings*, Cambridge: Peabody Museum Press, 1978.

Silverberg, Robert, *Mound Builders of Ancient America*, Greenwich: New York Graphic Society Ltd, 1968.

Thomas, Cyrus, *Mound Explorations*, Washington, D.C.: Smithsonian Institute Press, 1985.

Wright, Ronald, *Stolen Continents, the "New World" through Indian Eyes Since 1492*, Toronto: Viking Penguin, 1992.

Mounds of earth and shell

It is evening. A family is walking along a beach in Georgia, collecting shells that have washed in from the Atlantic Ocean. The family carries the shells – oyster, conch, clam and mussel – back from the shore to a low circular ridge. They then climb to the top where they have built a simple shelter where they live, away from the damp and mosquitoes of the tidal flats. The year is 2500 BC, and the family is doing what families have done for generations before them: adding shells from the shore and from food remains to build a mound. Millions of shells were needed.

During the next 3000 years, mound building went on across the eastern half of North America.

Further inland, earth was used instead of shells. These mounds in many shapes and sizes became centers of community life. Around some, large cities grew up. Some were a stage for elaborate religious ceremonies. Some supported temples. On top of others were the homes of rulers who were believed to be descended from the sun. But — most important for us — mounds were burial places for the dead. Most of what we can guess of the daily life of Native Americans before the Europeans arrived comes from these sites.

The mounds are proof that advanced cultures existed in ancient America that deserve our attention and respect.

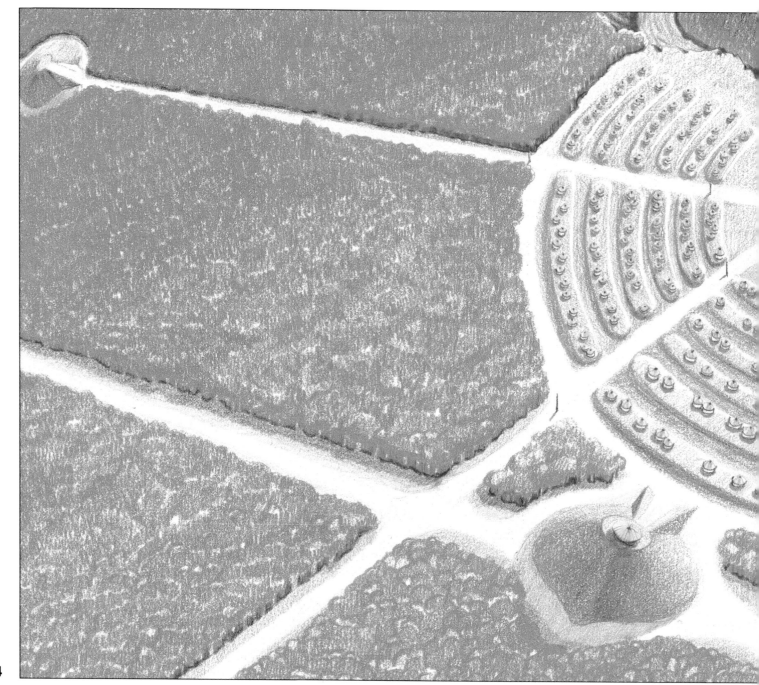

Half a million tons of earth were moved to build Poverty Point in Louisiana.

Avenues cut through circular ridges to the plaza. Was it a vast sun calendar?

The first mounds of earth

Tens of thousands of mounds made of earth have been found from Florida northwest to Ontario and Manitoba, and from the Atlantic west to the Mississippi River. Each mound is different and holds its own story. They vary in size from a few meters across to gigantic structures using tons of earth. They take many forms, from low hills to massive flat-topped pyramids. Some, known as effigy mounds, were shaped like animals, birds, serpents and humans.

The mounds were all built by hand, for the builders had no donkeys or horses, and no carts with wheels. Sticks loosened the earth which was then shoveled into baskets. The baskets were carried to the mounds, where the earth was dumped and stamped solid. In some mounds the earth was carefully layered with colored clays, ash and sand.

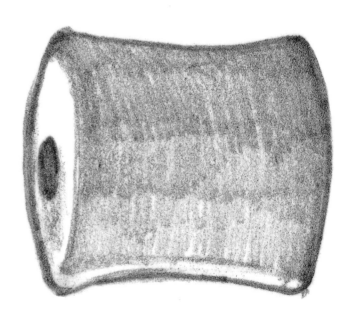

owl effigy bead,
Poverty Point, about 1500 BC

bannerstones found in
Kentucky, 3000 to 2000 BC

bannerstones helped balance an atlatl

Let us explore one of the earliest earthen structures in North America. It was built in northern Louisiana between 1700 and 870 BC, probably as a great religious center. Half a million tons of earth were moved in the construction. The final shape is complex. Six low ridges curve into a half circle nearly a mile across. A pyramid seven stories high is connected by a wide ramp to the outer ring.

Because avenues that cut through the ridges to the huge plaza, and postholes in the plaza itself, seem to mark the positions of the sun at different seasons of the year, some scientists believe the structure was a vast calendar.

Two thousand people seem to have lived here in simple thatched huts with outdoor cooking fires.

Buried in the mounds are objects made from hard stone that did not exist nearby and must have been brought from as far away as the Great Lakes, Florida or the Appalachian Mountains. Clay figurines resemble those made in Mexico. The site was occupied for more than 900 years.

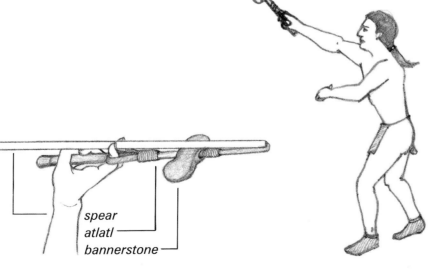

spear
atlatl
bannerstone

The atlatl was a stick with a hook at one end that helped hunters launch spears. It was held in one hand, much the same way javelins are held. The atlatl "lengthened" the arm of the hunter and increased the speed of the throw. It was used for more than 10,000 years until the arrival of the bow and arrow.

Mounds where the dead were buried with their personal possessions grew to

enormous sizes and reveal to us the elaborate cultures of ancient America.

Burial Mounds and the Adena

Around 1000 BC another group of mound builders emerged in the Ohio River valley. We do not know what they called themselves, but they were named the Adena people after the Ohio estate where a major mound was explored.

The Adena developed an impressive culture in the centuries that followed. We know it from changes in the way they buried their dead. They seem to have believed that the dead rejoined the community of those who had died before, but that a spirit remained which had to be guarded by special ceremonies.

In early Adena burial mounds, bodies were put in a shallow pit lined with clay and covered by bark; the grave was then covered with a small mound of earth. Sometimes, on the same site, bodies were cremated. Sometimes bodies were left exposed for several years. The bones were then collected, cleaned, placed in a bundle and buried. In some mounds, only parts of bodies have been found. Pottery, tools and pipes were buried with the dead. With each burial the mounds grew larger.

As centuries passed, ceremonies changed. Bodies of important persons were painted with red ochre and lay in state, while gifts and food were placed beside them. Sometimes a canopy was erected over an open tomb. Some tombs were lined with logs before being covered with earth.

Adena stone pipe, Ohio

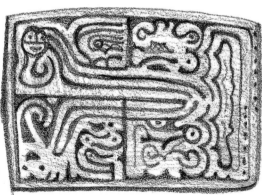

Adena stone tablet – possibly used to stamp designs on cloth or on bodies

Mounds grew to a tremendous size. Some built in groups were surrounded with high embankments. We think these sacred circles were ritual centers because of the variety of items found: antlered headdresses, effigy pipes, copper bracelets, jewelry, designs cut from sheets of mica, flat stone tablets covered with graceful designs, and polished enemy skulls.

Other sacred places were the effigy mounds. Only a few feet high, they were made in the shapes of birds, beasts, reptiles and men, and were thought to be inhabited by powerful spirits. The building of effigy mounds spread north from Louisiana to southern Ontario.

The Adena did not live on top of the mounds but in houses built in small groups nearby. The dwellings were circular in shape, the walls probably made of clay plastered over pole-frames.

Inside a cooking fire burned at the center and storage pits were dug in the floor. One house might shelter a single family or up to forty people.

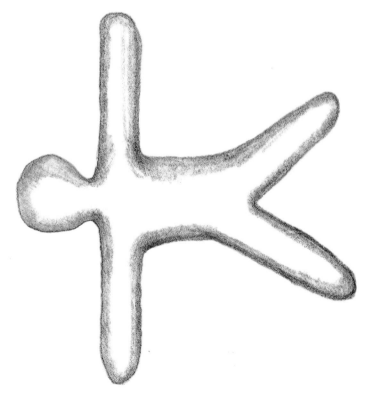

effigy mound, Wisconsin, 120 feet long (36 meters)

Serpent Mound, Rice Lake, Ontario, 180 feet long (60 meters) **11**

The Adena lived in round houses with walls made from clay over pole-frames.

Nearby, banks of earth surrounded sacred mounds where rituals took place.

Sacred spaces and the Hopewells

Around 100 BC changes took place in the land of the Adena. A new culture emerged that made the burial of the dead even more ritualistic. Burial mounds became massive with larger structures stretching out on all sides. These people have been called the Hopewells after another farm in Ohio where mounds were found.

Their burial mounds reached the height of seven-story buildings. Around these sacred spaces, elegant banks of earth were shaped into vast circles, squares and pentagons. And from these extended magnificent avenues, flanked by earthen walls.

The huge burial mounds seem to have been built by large numbers of people in one organized effort, rather than over many centuries and generations. They seem to have been meant only for the high-born and powerful members of the community. Sometimes bones were preserved in fine baskets in a temple on top of the mound.

The Hopewells also honored their ruler by sacrificing his wives and close advisers during the funeral ceremony. All were buried with him, along with his prized possessions, to accompany him on his voyage to the next world.

The Hopewells flourished for a few centuries and left us some magnificent constructions. For reasons that are still unclear, around AD 400 the Hopewells stopped building mounds as their culture changed.

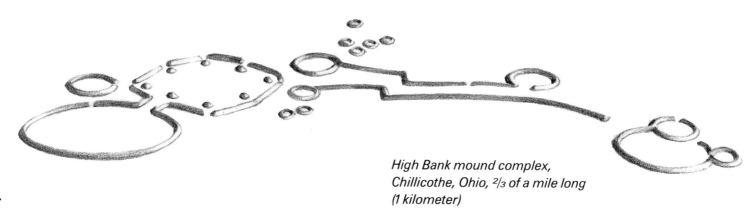

High Bank mound complex, Chillicothe, Ohio, 2/3 of a mile long (1 kilometer)

Temple building and the Mississippians

The next great surge of mound building began around AD 800. It emerged in the southern states and as far west as Oklahoma, particularly in the central and lower Mississippi valley.

Although the Mississippians built mounds for the dead, we are more impressed by the towns that surrounded them. From a huge central plaza, causeways or log stairs led up to a four-sided pyramid with a flat top. The largest towns had a dozen such flat-topped mounds and smaller cone-shaped burial mounds. Some mounds held large thatch-roofed temples, or buildings for preserving the bodies or bones of the dead. Other mounds supported the homes of the ruler and his high officials.

The towns were both religious and trade centers. Public granaries guaranteed food during famine. High stockades offered protection. On the plazas, ceremonial games were held.

Because Native cultures in the Mississippi valley survived through the 17th century, we know something of them from historic documents. Some were sun worshippers. The Natchez believed their leader had descended from the sun, and even called him "Sun." Humans were sacrificed when a Sun died. The eldest son of the Sun's sister became the new ruler.

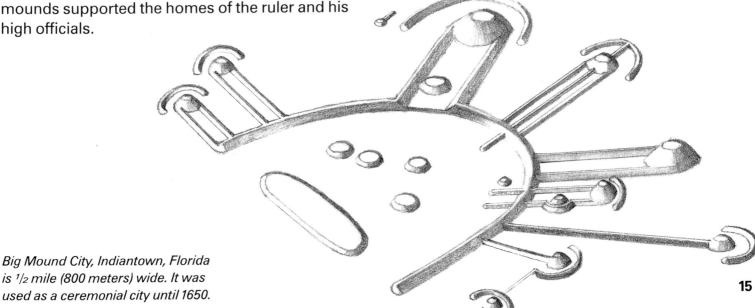

Big Mound City, Indiantown, Florida is 1/2 mile (800 meters) wide. It was used as a ceremonial city until 1650.

In the Mississippi valley, large towns developed and temples built on mounds

preserved the bones of rulers believed to have descended from the sun.

Let us visit a town of the Mississippians.

You are in the center of a huge plaza, more than twice the size of a football field. Ahead is a pyramid with four sides and a flat top. A wide ramp leads up to a magnificently decorated temple.

On its thatched roof are carvings of sacred birds, standing out like huge weathervanes. Inside the temple is a wooden box containing a stone figure and the remains of a ruler who was believed to be related to the sun, and sent to earth to head a family of rulers.

On the opposite side of the square the Sun's residence sits on a smaller pyramid. Its clay walls are covered with cane mats. On the ground below are smaller dwellings for the people. Around them, crowded within the walls of the town, are drying racks, gardens, warehouses, public and family granaries. Outside the walls, a river links the town with others hundreds of miles away.

People gather in the plaza to watch games. Lacrosse originated here. Known as the "little brother of war," it was sometimes used to settle disputes between villages. Chunkey was another popular game. A stone disk was rolled and a javelin was thrown to the spot where the disk was likely to stop. Everyone in town came to gamble on the results.

basic pyramid types
(based on the drawings of William Morgan)

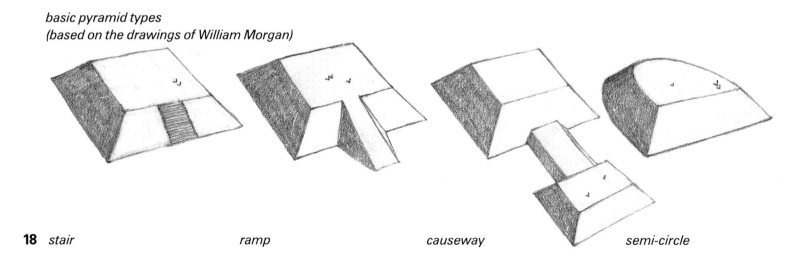

stair *ramp* *causeway* *semi-circle*

Rituals included the drinking of the purifying "black drink." Warriors drank it before leaving to fight. Leaders drank it before deciding matters of state. At the summer corn festival all fires in the village were put out. After purification ceremonies, new fires were lit and disputes forgiven. Boys entering manhood got new names.

From time to time, mounds were enlarged during celebrations. Excavations reveal beautifully made objects: cats, serpents, sunbursts and sun circles, weeping eyes, eyes on open hands, hands with a cross on the palm and elaborate crosses symbolizing the sacred fire.

These people were the ancestors of the Creeks, Cherokees, Choctaws and Chickasaws. Although their culture was in decline when Columbus arrived, journals of the early European visitors tell of clean, orderly towns, of leaders wearing feathered headdresses being carried on litters. They also describe deserted villages and houses full of the dead, probably victims of diseases brought from Europe.

three-headed pottery vessel, Tennessee

ceramic bottle, Arkansas

embossed copper plate design, Etowah, Georgia

19

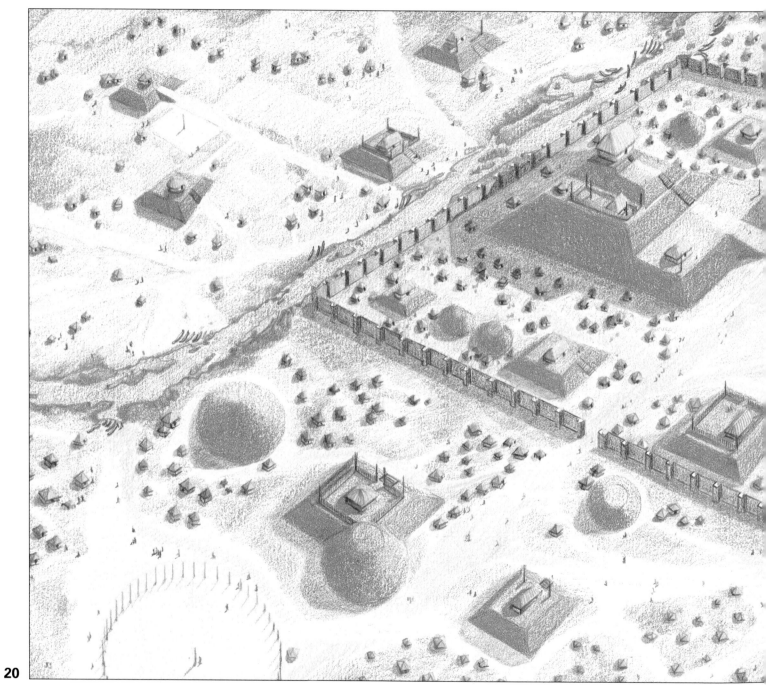

Cahokia in Illinois, the largest town built before the Europeans arrived, had

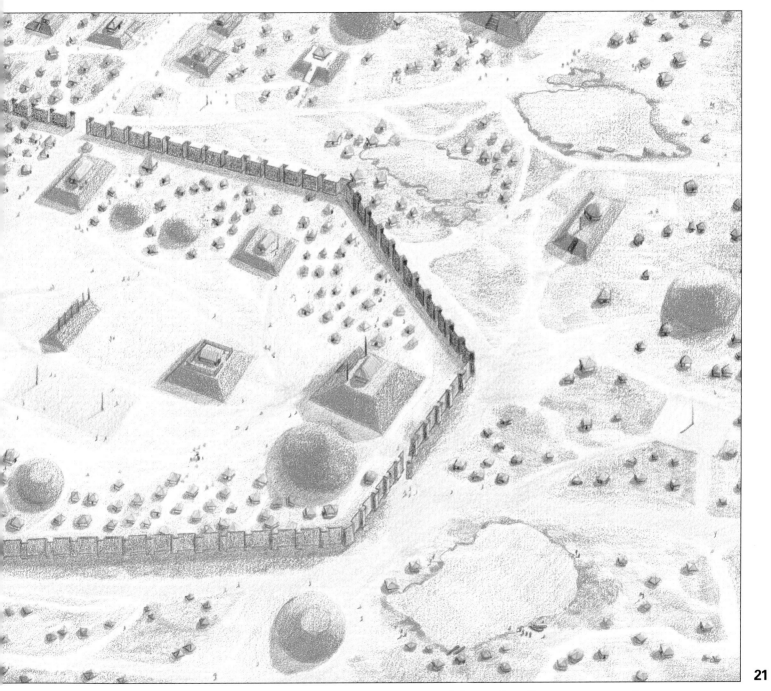

10,000 people, 120 mounds, a ten-story pyramid and a forty-acre plaza.

Cahokia — a huge town

The most astonishing town built by the Mississippians was Cahokia. It was bigger than any town built north of Mexico before the Europeans arrived. At its height around the year AD 1100, it supported a population of 10,000. Located on the rich bottom land across the Mississippi River from present-day St. Louis, it was a bustling trade center with ties to one-third of America.

Throughout the city loomed more than 120 mounds. The largest was a four-sided pyramid rising ten stories high from a base covering sixteen acres. Archaeologists believe it was built in fourteen phases.

Each time it was enlarged, the temple on top was rebuilt. The last temple was 100 feet (30 meters) long and probably four stories high. Its walls of mud plaster were three feet thick. Inside lived the supreme ruler tended by his priests. He looked down on the busy city below, with its plazas, docks and warehouses.

Directly in front of this pyramid was a forty-acre plaza — the largest of six major plazas — where important religious ceremonies took place. Nearby a woodhenge, or sun calendar circle, was created by placing a series of large posts in a wide circle. An astronomer-priest could stand on a lookout at the exact center and observe how the sun rose and set in relationship to the posts. From this he could calculate the time of year most favorable to plant and harvest.

pottery figure of mother and child, possibly used as a water bottle

Cahokia birdman tablet of warrior with a nose of a falcon

ceremonial wooden bowl with rattle in head

The downtown section of the city where the ruling classes lived was surrounded by a double stockade, guarded by archers from sentry boxes. The wall was rebuilt four times during the 200 years when Cahokia was most influential. Pyramids were also built outside the walls where the common people seem to have lived.

The aristocracy were buried in mounds shaped like cones. One such mound contained 250 bodies.

The skeleton of a powerful ruler lies face down on a blanket made from 10,000 mussel and conch shell beads. The body is surrounded by three males and three females. All were between seventeen and twenty-one years of age, and all were buried at the same time.

By 1400 Cahokia's population had dwindled to four or five thousand. When the French came through a few centuries later, nothing was left but overgrown mounds.

Had the soil been exhausted? Had weather changes caused famine? Had disease broken out? Was the rule of the sun king too harsh? These are the mysteries that make the study of Cahokia so fascinating.

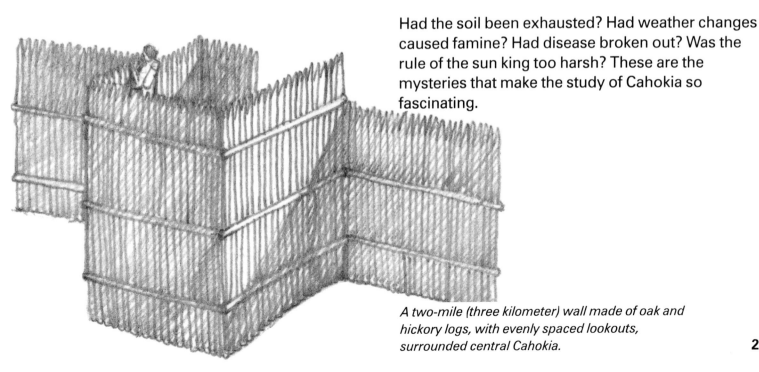

A two-mile (three kilometer) wall made of oak and hickory logs, with evenly spaced lookouts, surrounded central Cahokia.

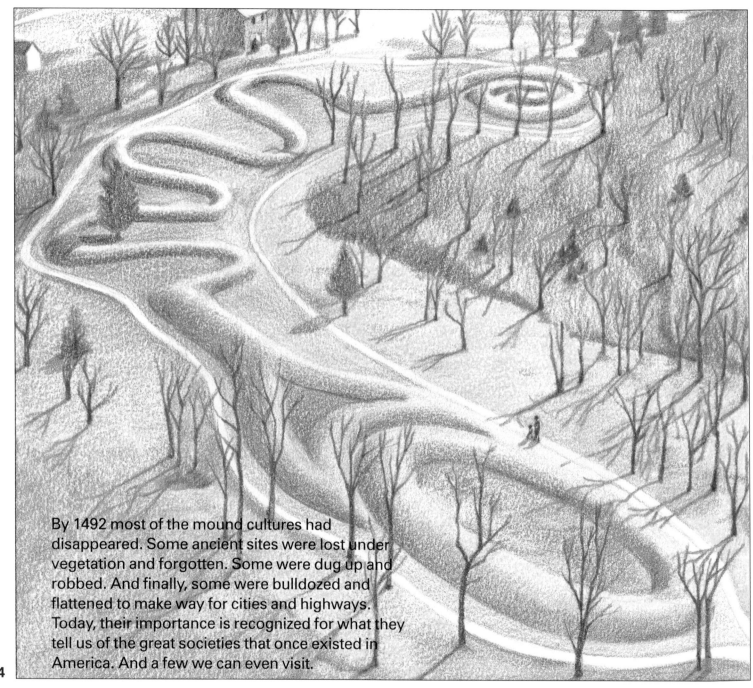

By 1492 most of the mound cultures had disappeared. Some ancient sites were lost under vegetation and forgotten. Some were dug up and robbed. And finally, some were bulldozed and flattened to make way for cities and highways. Today, their importance is recognized for what they tell us of the great societies that once existed in America. And a few we can even visit.

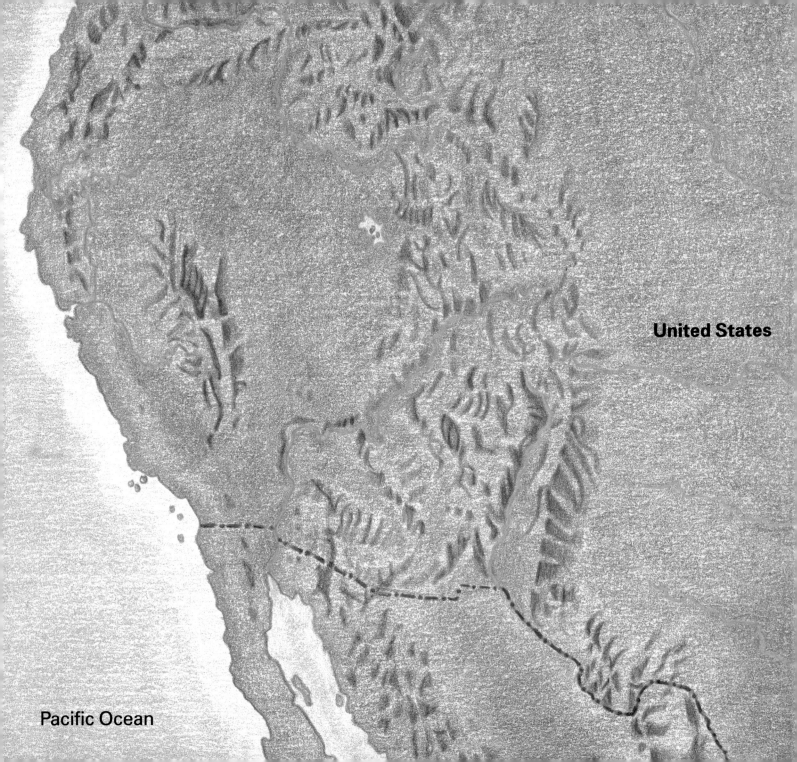

United States

Pacific Ocean

Canada

Ohio River

Mississippi River

Atlantic Ocean

Gulf of Mexico